AF477905

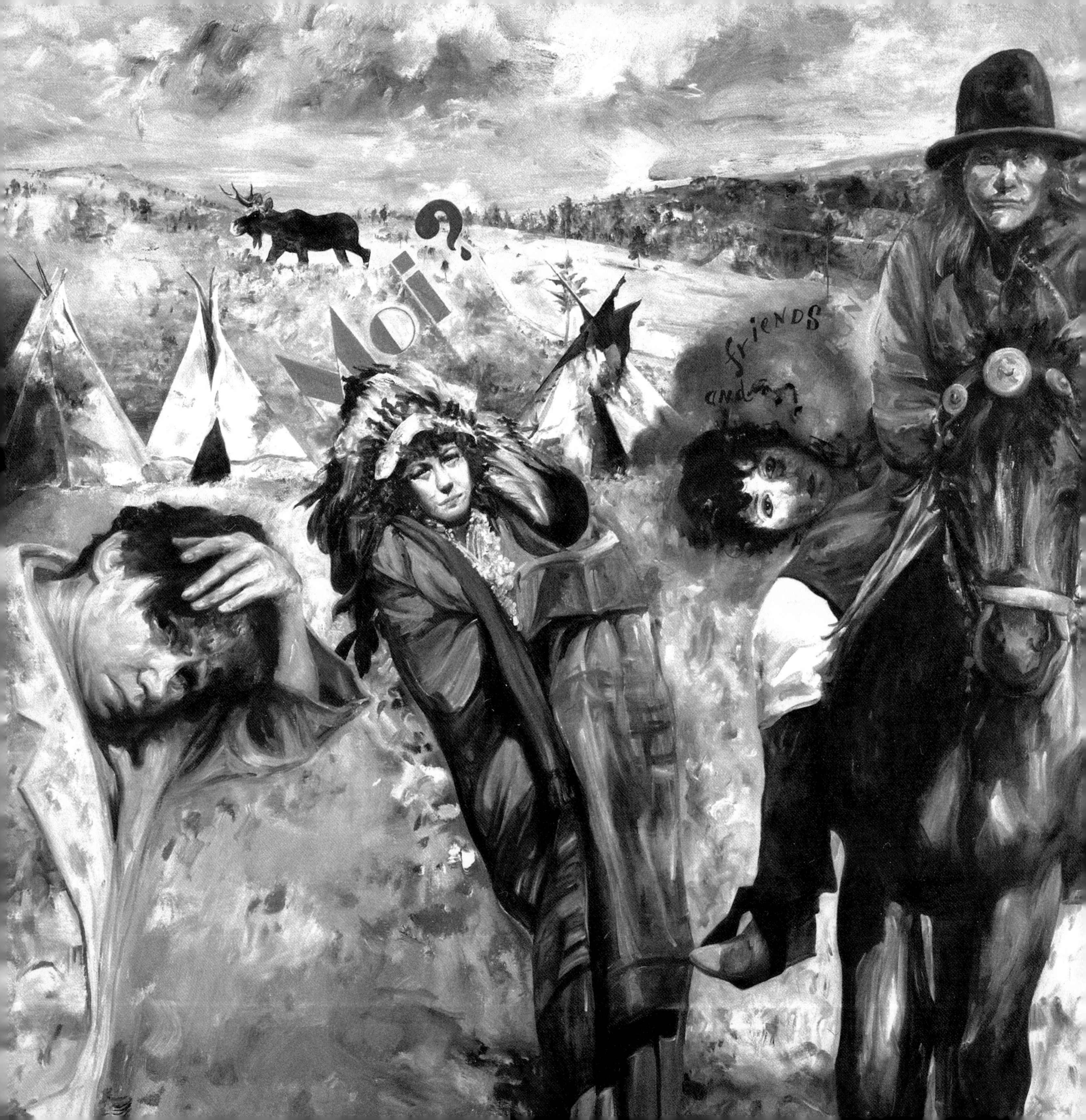
friends
and

Joyce Treiman
Friends and Strangers

Guest
Curators
Maurice Bloch and Grant Holcomb

Fisher Gallery, University of Southern California
January 20, 1988 to February 27, 1988

Memorial Art Gallery, University of Rochester
May 3, 1988 to June 12, 1988

Portland Art Museum
July 5, 1988 to August 21, 1988

Organized by the Fisher Gallery, University of Southern California
Selma Holo, Director

ACKNOWLEDGMENT

The Fisher Gallery gratefully acknowledges Alan D. Levy for his special support of the catalogue, *Joyce Treiman: Friends and Strangers.* We are also grateful to Joyce Treiman's dealers, Sally Fairweather and Shirley Hardin of Fairweather Hardin Gallery, Penny Schmidt and Alice Bingham of Schmidt-Bingham Gallery, and Mallory Freeman and Louis Leithold of Tortue Gallery for their support of the exhibition and catalogue. Maurice Bloch and Grant Holcomb, co-curators of the exhibition, brought insight, dedication and felicity of expression to the interpretation of the artist's work, and I extend my sincere thanks to both of them. Gordon Gilkey deserves our acknowledgment of his ongoing support and involvement with this exhibition and with the artist's life. The lenders, each of whom is named in the checklist, have been most generous. Without their cooperation the exhibition would not have been possible. I am also grateful to Jack Carter for his inspired design of the catalogue and installation. Fran Luban's superb video enhances the understanding and we are very grateful to her for its creation. And, to my staff, Kay Allen, Georgia Freedman-Harvey, Philo Northrup, and Greyling Peoples, I extend my deepest thanks. It is your dedicated support that makes efforts such as this possible at our University.

Selma Holo
Director
Fisher Gallery

Joyce Treiman's value as an artist is confined neither to her exquisite draftsmanship nor to her luscious painting. Rather, it also encompasses her profound and quirky vision of the world, one which she will articulate eloquently and acerbically at the drop of a hat. I first came to recognize this special combination of qualities years ago, early in our acquaintance. Joyce had invited me to see her latest work, an ongoing privilege which I had come to treasure. As had become our habit we perused her eclectic art collection before venturing into the studio. On that particular visit I could not help noticing that an exquisite little 1892 Vuillard painting was missing. "Oh, you're right", she responded to my inquiry after it. "I used it up".

Never in all my years as a curator had I heard such a blasphemous phrase about a work of art. Nor had I, on the other hand, ever been so unpretentiously made to bear witness to the volatile dialogue that can exist between a contemporary artist and the past. I was and continue to be stunned by Treiman's tenacious engagement with and absolute independence of the work of the masters. *Joyce Treiman: Friends and Strangers* celebrates her long and fruitful relationship with them in figurative paintings and drawings from the years 1967 to 1987. The exhibition does not even attempt to cover the artist's sculpture and prints or her work in the genres of landscape and still life. But if it did, the additional work would only be a more striking revelation of the uniqueness of her talent.

Joyce Treiman, then, by means of art *and* life, reminds us along with Yeats that soul can "clap its hands and sing for every tatter in its mortal dress". She challenged us to remember, long before it was fashionable to do so, that rich and lasting originality stems from the carefully cultivated understanding of where and when to jump off the train of our collective memory into uncharted terrain. It is a great pleasure to be able to claim responsibility for the Fisher Gallery for the origination and organization of *Friends and Strangers*. Thank you, Joyce Treiman, for allowing us the privilege of doing that work.

Selma Holo
Director
Fisher Gallery

JOYCE TREIMAN CHRONOLOGY

Born: Evanston, Illinois. May 29, 1922
Attended: Stephens College, Columbia, Missouri
University of Iowa, B.F.A. 1943
Lives and works in Los Angeles, California

Selected one-artist exhibitions

1942 Paul Theobald Gallery, Chicago, IL
1945 John Snowden Gallery, Chicago, IL
1947 The Art Institute of Chicago, IL
1950 Fairweather Garnett Gallery, Evanston, IL
Edwin Hewitt Gallery, New York, NY
1952 Palmer House Galleries, Chicago, IL
1953 Elizabeth Nelson Gallery, Chicago, IL
1955 Cliff Dwellers Club, Chicago, IL
Charles Feingarten Gallery, Chicago, IL
Fairweather Hardin Gallery, Chicago, IL; exhibitions also 1958, 1962, 1964, 1972, 1973, 1978, 1982, 1984, 1986
(Catalogue: *Treiman/Sculpture/Paintings*, 1964)
1960 Willard Gallery, New York, NY
(Catalogue: *Joyce Treiman, Guest Exhibition)*
1961 Felix Landau Gallery, Los Angeles, CA; exhibition also 1964
(Catalogue: *Paintings & Sculpture/ Joyce Treiman*, 1964)
1963 Forum Gallery, New York, NY; exhibitions also 1966, 1971, 1975, 1981
(Catalogue: *Joyce Treiman*, 1963)
1969 Adele Bednarz Gallery, Los Angeles, CA; exhibitions also 1971, 1974, 1976
1972/1973 La Jolla Museum of Contemporary Art, La Jolla, CA
(Catalogue: *Joyce Treiman Paintings)*
Telfair Academy of Arts and Sciences, Savannah, GA
1977 Traveling exhibition
Palos Verdes Art Center, Palos Verdes, CA
(Catalogue: *Joyce Treiman: The Model in the Studio)*
California State College, Long Beach, CA
Loyola Marymount University, Los Angeles, CA
University of California, Santa Cruz, CA
1978 Municipal Art Gallery, Los Angeles, CA
(Catalogue: *Joyce Treiman Retrospective, 1947–1977)*
James Willis Gallery, San Francisco, CA
Tortue Gallery, Santa Monica, CA; exhibitions also 1979, 1980, 1983, 1981, 1984, 1986
(Catalogue: *Joyce Treiman/Paintings*, 1983)
1979 The Art Institute of Chicago, IL
(Catalogue: *Drawings by Joyce Treiman)*
Grunwald Center for the Graphic Arts, UCLA, Los Angeles, CA
1982 California State University, San Jose, CA
Portland Art Museum, Portland, OR
1985 Santa Barbara Museum of Art, Santa Barbara, CA
1986 Schmidt-Bingham Gallery, New York, NY

Selected group exhibitions

1945 *The Forty-ninth Exhibition by Artists of Chicago and Vicinity*, The Art Institute of Chicago, IL exhibitions (annual), also 1946 to 1959.
1948 *Contemporary American Paintings*, Virginia Museum of Fine Arts, Richmond, VA
1950 *Young American Artists*, The Metropolitan Museum of Art, New York, NY
Contemporary American Painting and Sculpture, Krannert Art Museum, University of Illinois, Urbana, IL exhibitions (annual), also 1951, 1952, 1956, 1957, 1961, 1963, 1965, 1967, 1969, 1971, 1974
1951 *Annual Exhibition of American Painting*, Whitney Museum of American Art, New York, NY exhibitions (annual), also 1952, 1953, 1958, 1961
1953 *Contemporary American Paintings*, John Herron Art Museum, Indianapolis, IN
1955 *Carnegie International Exhibition*, Carnegie Institute, Pittsburgh, PA, exhibitions (annual), also 1957
1958 *Catalogue of the 153rd Annual Exhibition*, Pennsylvania Academy of the Fine Arts, Philadelphia, PA
1961 *Annual California Painting and Sculpture Exhibition*, La Jolla Museum of Contemporary Art, La Jolla, CA
1962 *Recent Painting U.S.A.*, The Museum of Modern Art, New York, NY
Lithographs from the Tamarind Workshop, Art Galleries, University of California, Los Angeles, CA
1962/1963 *Fifty California Artists* (traveling exhibition organized by the San Francisco Museum of Art), Whitney Museum of American Art, New York, NY; Walker Art Center, Minneapolis, MN; Albright-Knox Art Gallery, Buffalo, NY; Des Moines Art Center, Des Moines, IA

1965 *Far West Regional Exhibition of Art Across America*, San Francisco Museum of Art, San Francisco, CA

1966 *Seven California Figurative Artists*, Palm Springs Desert Museum, Palm Springs, CA
Contemporary Art: The Human Image, Montgomery Art Gallery, Scripps College, Claremont, CA

1969 *Tamarind: Homage to Lithography*, Museum of Modern Art, New York, NY

1972 *147th Annual Exhibition*, National Academy of Design, New York, NY exhibitions (annual), also 1973, 1986

1974 *Exhibitions of Paintings Eligible for Childe Hassam Fund Purchase*, The American Academy of Arts and Letters, New York, NY exhibitions (annual), also 1975, 1976

1975 *Impetus the Creative Process*, Municipal Art Gallery, Los Angeles, CA

1976 *Contemporary Monotypes*, The Santa Barbara Museum of Art, Santa Barbara, CA

1977 *Invitational Annual*, San Francisco Art Institute, San Francisco, CA

1978 *Contemporary American Monotypes*, Smithsonian Institution, Washington, D.C.

1979 *American Portrait Drawing*, National Portrait Gallery, Smithsonian Institution, Washington, D.C.

1980 *100 Artists—100 Years*, The Art Institute of Chicago, Chicago, IL

1981 *Alternative Realities*, University Art Gallery, University of Minnesota, Minneapolis, MN
Portraits in Miniature, Fisher Gallery, University of Southern California, Los Angeles, CA
Southern California Artists 1940–1980, Laguna Beach Museum of Art, Laguna Beach, CA

1982 *Los Angeles Art in Nagoya, Japan*, Nagoya City Museum, Japan
Drawings by Painters, Long Beach Museum of Art, Long Beach, CA

1983 *Twentieth Century Drawings Acquired Since 1958*, The Art Institute of Chicago, Chicago, IL

1984 *Ceci n'est pas le surrealisme: California: Idioms of Surrealism*, Fisher Gallery, University of Southern California, Los Angeles, CA

1984/1985 *Twentieth Century American Drawings: The Figure in Context* (traveling exhibition), Terra Museum of American Art, Evanston, IL; Arkansas Art Center, Little Rock, AR; Oklahoma Art Center, Oklahoma City, OK; Toledo Museum of Art, Toledo, OH; Elvehjem Museum of Art, University of Wisconsin, Madison, WI; National Academy of Design, New York, NY

1987 *Contemporary California Artists*, Taipei Museum, Taipei, Taiwan

Public collections

Abbott Laboratories, North Chicago, IL
Allen Memorial Art Museum, Oberlin, OH
Arkansas Art Center, Little Rock, AR
The Art Institute of Chicago, IL
Atlantic Richfield, Los Angeles, CA
Ball State University, Muncie, IN
California State University, Northridge, CA
Claremont Colleges, Claremont, CA
Denver Art Museum, Denver, CO
Home Federal Savings and Loan Association, Los Angeles, CA
Illinois State Museum, Springfield, IL
International Minerals and Chemical Corporation, Northbrook, IL
Kemper Insurance Company, Chicago, IL
Long Beach Museum of Art, Long Beach, CA
Los Angeles County Museum of Art, Los Angeles, CA
Metropolitan Museum of Art, New York, NY
Museum of Modern Art, New York, NY
National Gallery of Art, Washington, D.C.
Norton Simon Museum, Pasadena, CA
Oakland Museum, Oakland, CA
Pasadena Art Museum, Pasadena, CA
Philbrook Art Center, Tulsa, OK
Portland Museum, Portland, OR
Memorial Art Gallery, Rochester, NY
Santa Barbara Museum of Art, Santa Barbara, CA
Security Pacific National Bank, Los Angeles, CA
State University of Iowa, Iowa City, IA
University of California, Los Angeles, CA
University of California, Santa Cruz, CA
University of Illinois, Champaign, IL
University of Oregon, Eugene, OR
Utah State University, Logan, UT
Whitney Museum of American Art, New York, NY

For Joyce Treiman drawing is a primary impulse of her art. Throughout a substantial career as a painter, drawing has always been at the heart of her work. Treiman's draughtsmanship displays a control of line, tone, and color that first evolved when she was enrolled as a child in Chicago's Academy of Fine Arts, and continued later at the Art Institute. She has drawn unceasingly ever since, but her drawings still reflect the ideals of the traditional training she received at that time. A fine, linear quality still provides the monumentality of her work in pencil although the rich, painterly use of color and tone that characterizes the production of recent years is most clearly revealed in her drawings in pastel and charcoal. Pastel comes closer to painting than any other graphic medium, while charcoal permits a sweep and power of intimate expression many artists prefer over other techniques.

Treiman enjoys the flexibility of drawing and finds fulfillment in a diversity and freedom in the medium that painting less often offers an artist. Although thumbnail sketches may supply first thoughts for a major picture, they actually serve Treiman more than a transitory need. Even the recognizable preparatory studies for paintings in this exhibition can be more appropriately designated autonomous drawings. Such drawings are free and fully developed interpretations or variations of a given theme imbued with a vibrant, independent life of their own. Clearly an extension of her painting, drawings of this nature provide an important outlet for the energy and flow of ideas that continually command the attention and guide the hand of an intensely creative mind.

The variety Treiman brings to her work defies the analytic methodology of contemporary criticism, I suspect intentionally, since she has been made so actively aware of a new wave of scholarship which struggles to seize every available opportunity to bypass the more elusive creative impulse in search of more provocative meaning, more than usually an artist's life-style. Deliberately avoiding sensationalism of any kind, Treiman is best described as a sympathetic and expressive observer of the human condition who is at times a romantic, and almost always autobiographical in a somewhat nostalgic way.

Although Treiman's achievement in painting and drawing suggests great facility, there is nothing frivolous about it; it is much more the end result of a carefully orchestrated use of the artistic means she manipulates with such seeming ease. Like Degas, one of the masters she admires, Treiman is uncompromising in her effort to approximate reality and interpret those manifold aspects of life which fascinate her most—exotic Vegas dancers, the so-called "jokers", or the studio models that so often include herself, a ready-made prop assuming the role of protagonist. In the remarkable series of portraits of Rose, her mother, a daughter's devotion still continues to reach for a deeper insight into a significant part of her life.

Treiman's debt to masters like Rembrandt, Tiepolo, Goya, Turner, Eakins, Sargent, Monet, Bonnard and Degas has been far too much overplayed and recited by critics. Although she remains faithful to the basic tenets of some of those painters of the past, and some of her suggestive power is unquestionably derived ultimately from them, it must be emphasized that she is above all an individual artist in her own right who cannot be identified with them beyond the homage she so readily acknowledges.

In short, Treiman's art can best be characterized as compelling, versatile, yet always unpretentious. It is an art exhibiting great style and conviction concerned with concepts of form and coherent design that make deeply felt images and ideas come vividly to life on canvas and paper. Her drawings are often mesmerizing, attracting an ever-widening audience of devoted followers and collectors but, even more significantly, through the drawings alone she can claim the distinction of being one of the very few artists other artists admire and respect.

Maurice Bloch
Professor Emeritus
University of California,
Los Angeles

PORTRAIT OF B.D.
Charcoal and chalk
1977, 30×22
Courtesy of the Artist

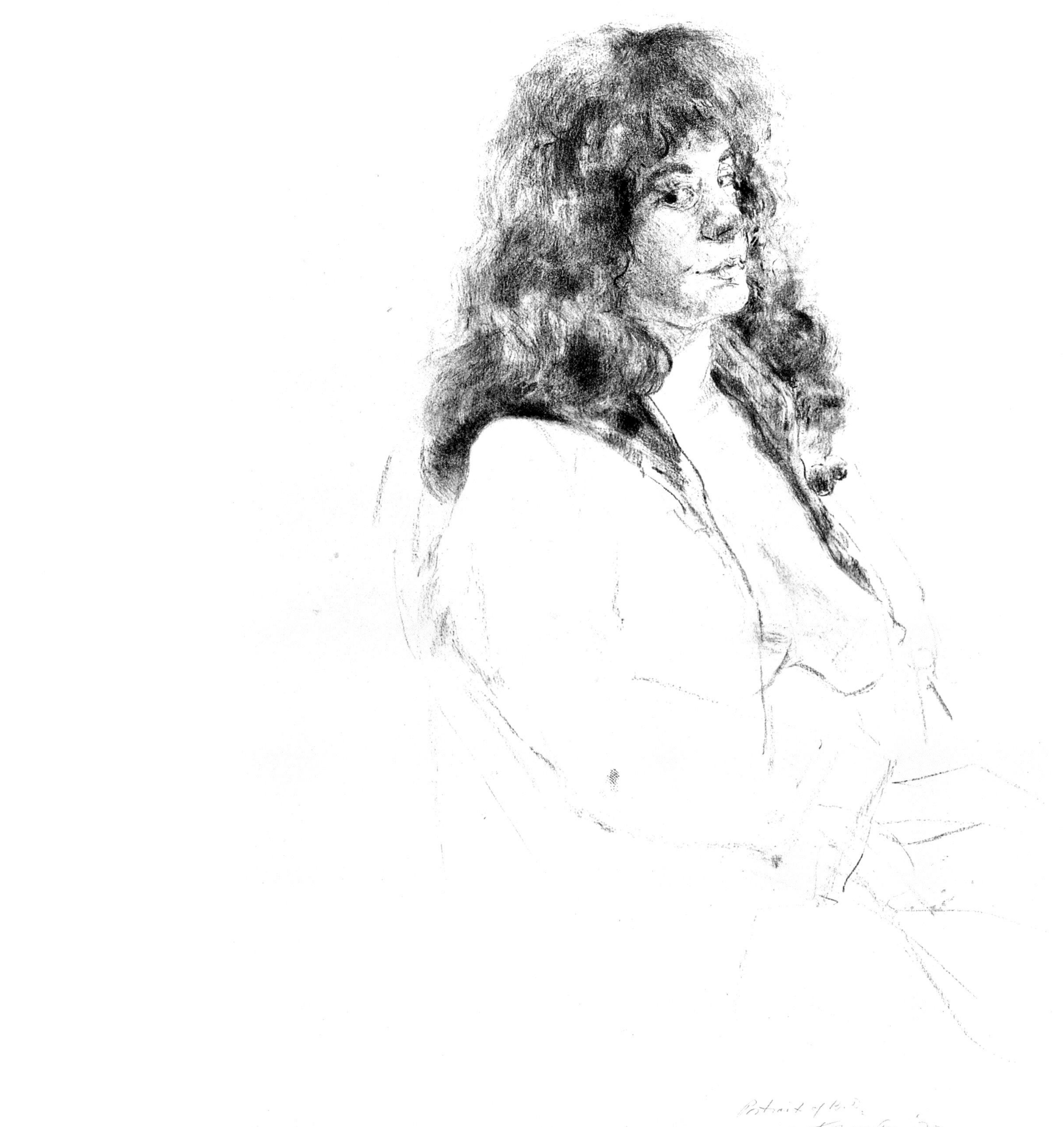
Portrait of

STUDY FOR TURNER AND ME
Pencil and ink
1978, 30½ × 22¼
Courtesy of Fairweather Hardin Gallery
Chicago, Illinois

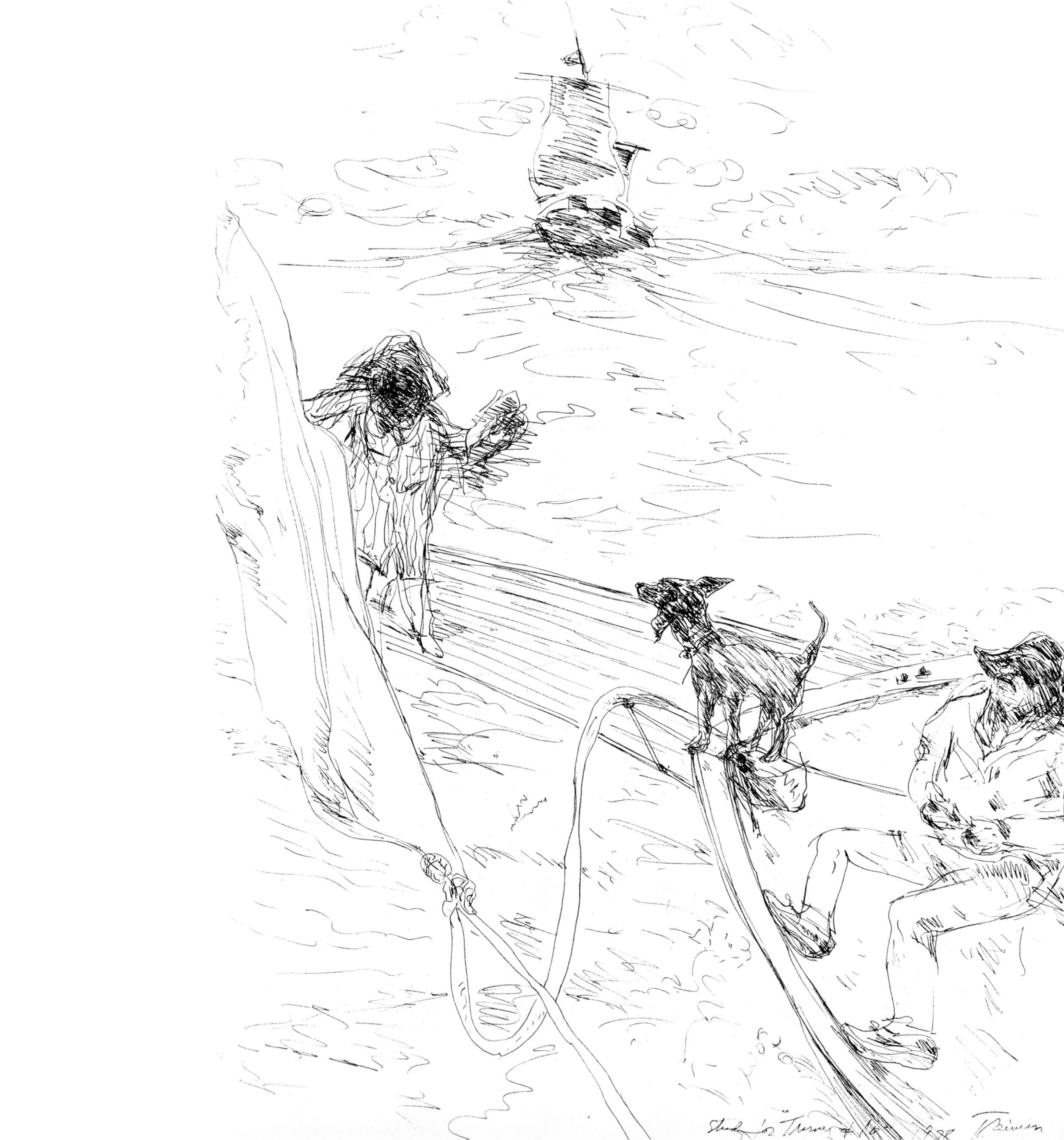

MAN IN BLUE DERBY
Pastel on black paper
1980, 23½ × 17½
Courtesy of Tortue Gallery
Santa Monica, California

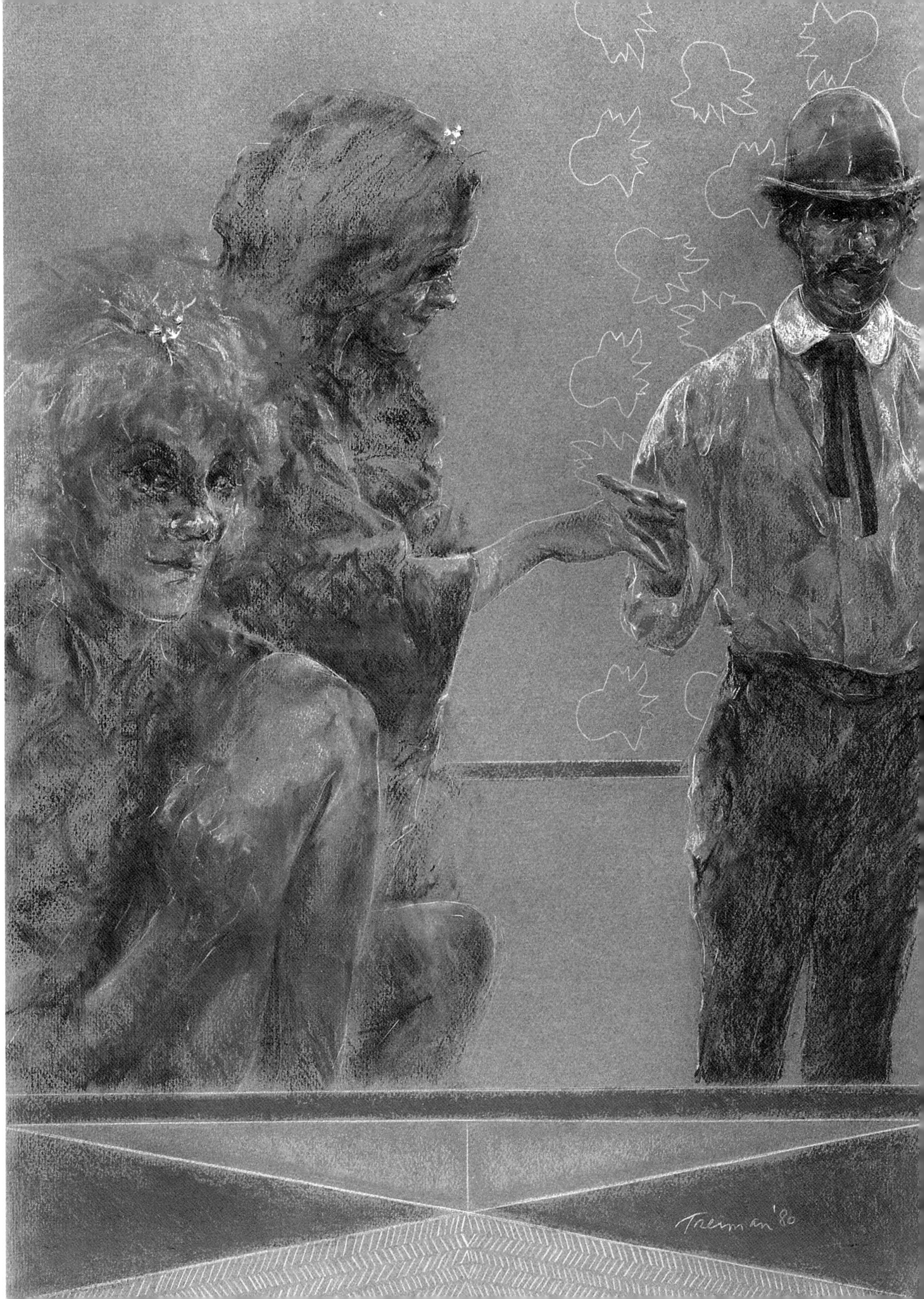

PLUMED HELMET (STUDY FOR THE PARTING)
Pencil and pastel
1982, 30¼ × 21¾
Collection of Memorial Art Gallery
of the University of Rochester, New York;
Anonymous Gift

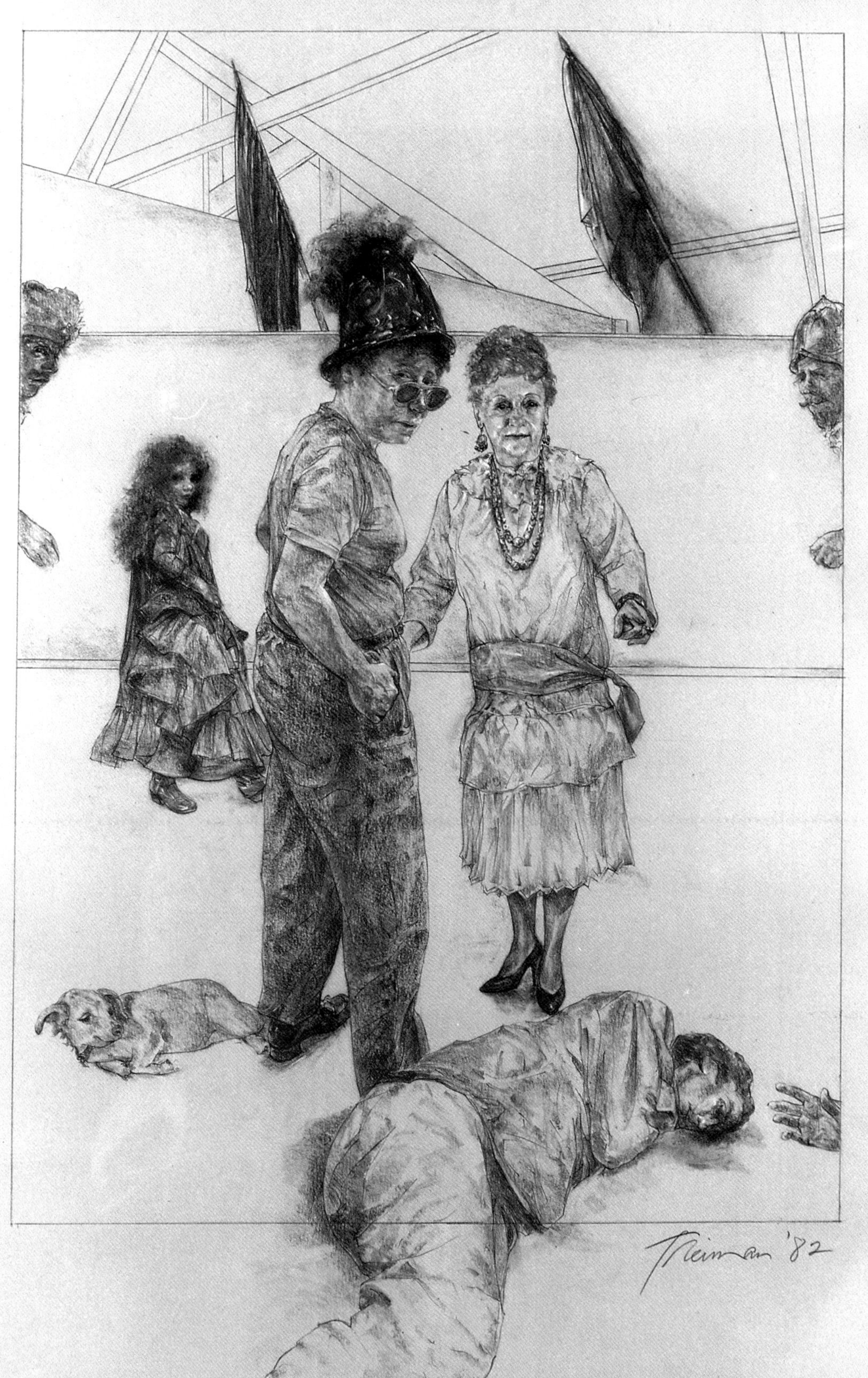
Treiman '82

THE ROCK AND THE RAM
Charcoal, pastel, pencil and colored pencils
1984, 18 × 15
Courtesy of Schmidt-Bingham Gallery
New York, New York

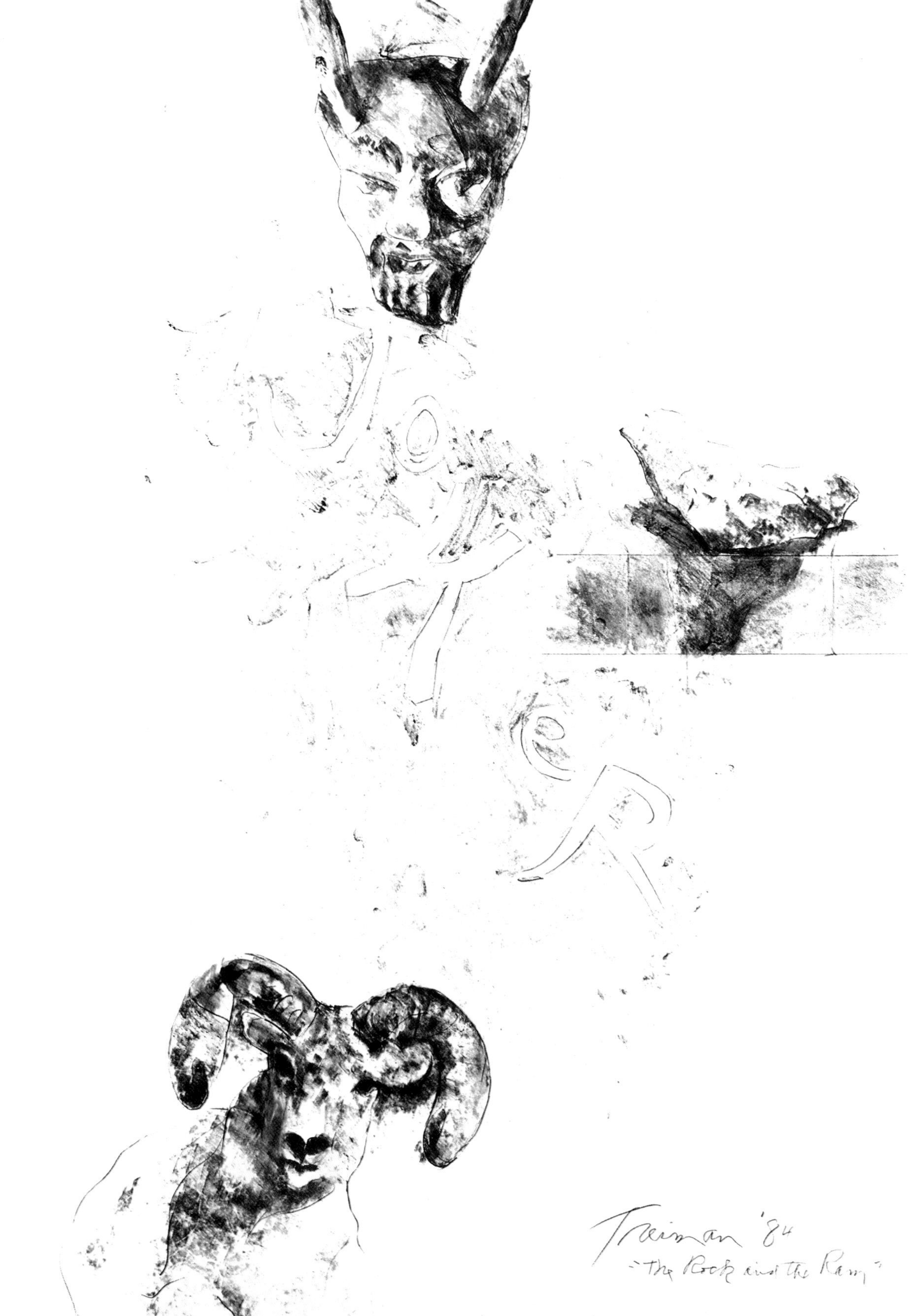
Treiman '84
"The Rock and the Ram"

ROSE IX
Pastel and charcoal
1985, 30 × 22
Collection of Judith Taylor
Los Angeles, California

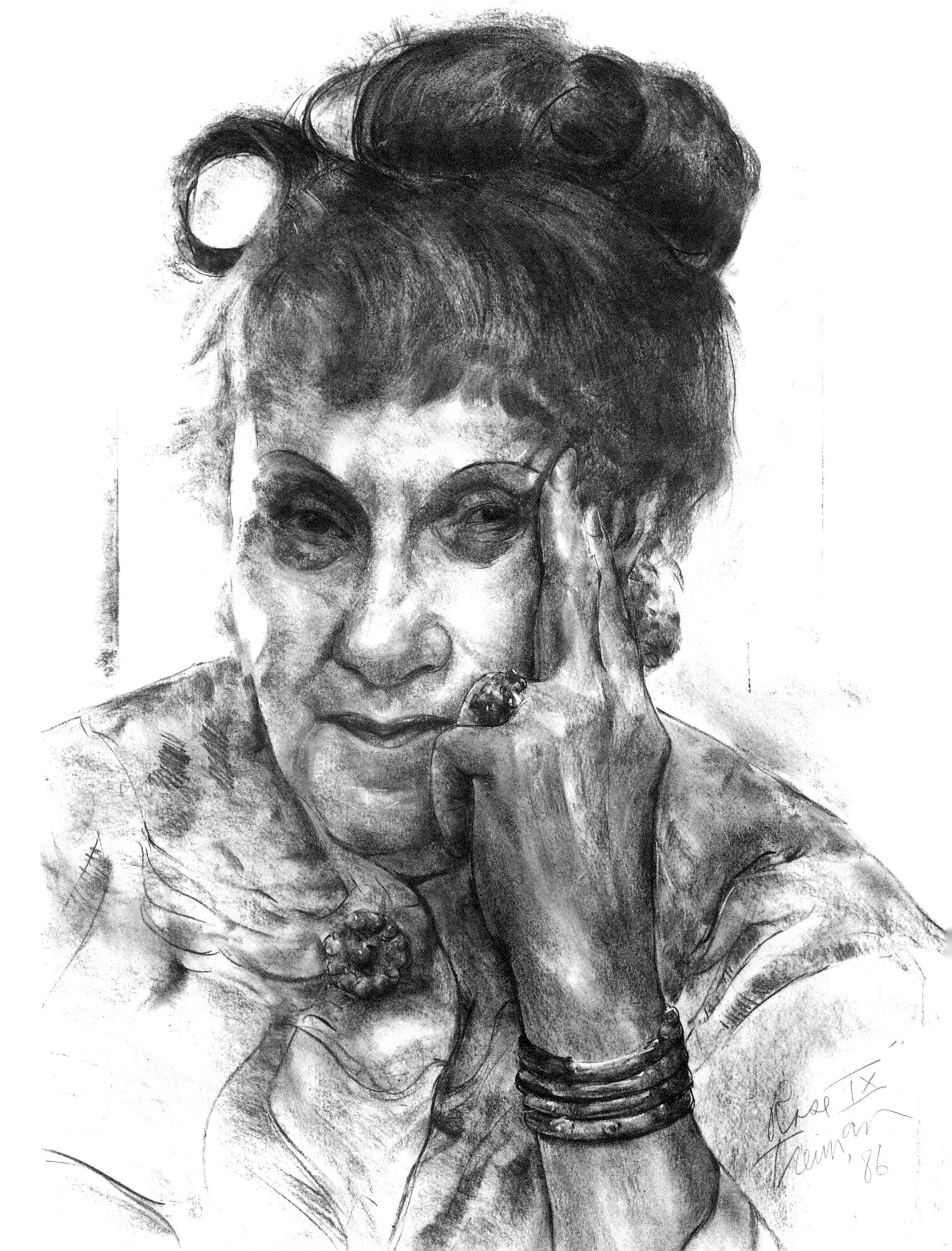
Rose IX
Treiman, '86

ROSE X
Pastel and charcoal
1986, 30 × 22
Collection of Donald M. Treiman
Los Angeles, California

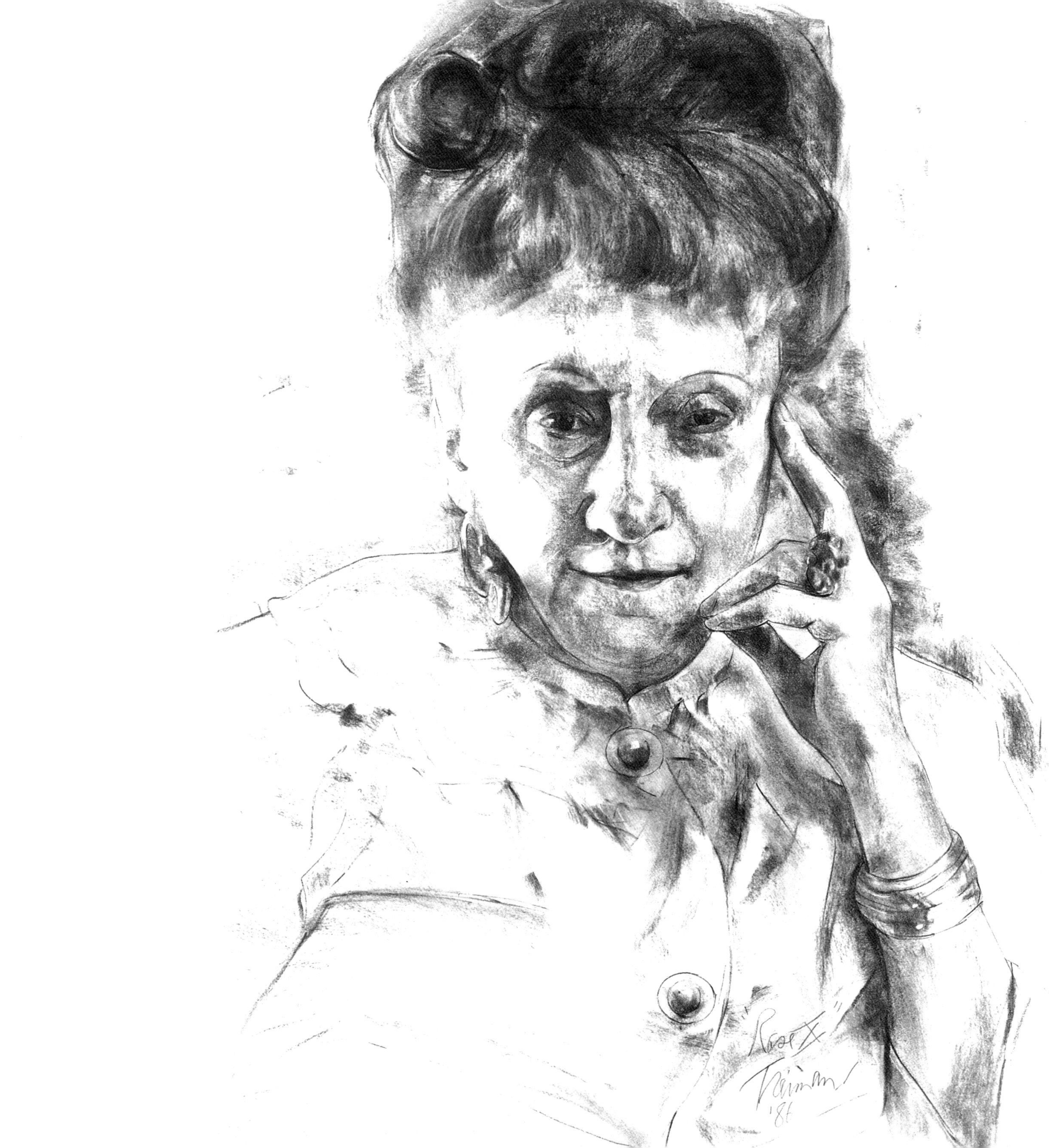

NUDE AND HEAD STUDY FOR
THE PAINTING "THE NUDE OUT WEST"
Charcoal, pastel, pencil and ink
1986–87
Courtesy of the artist

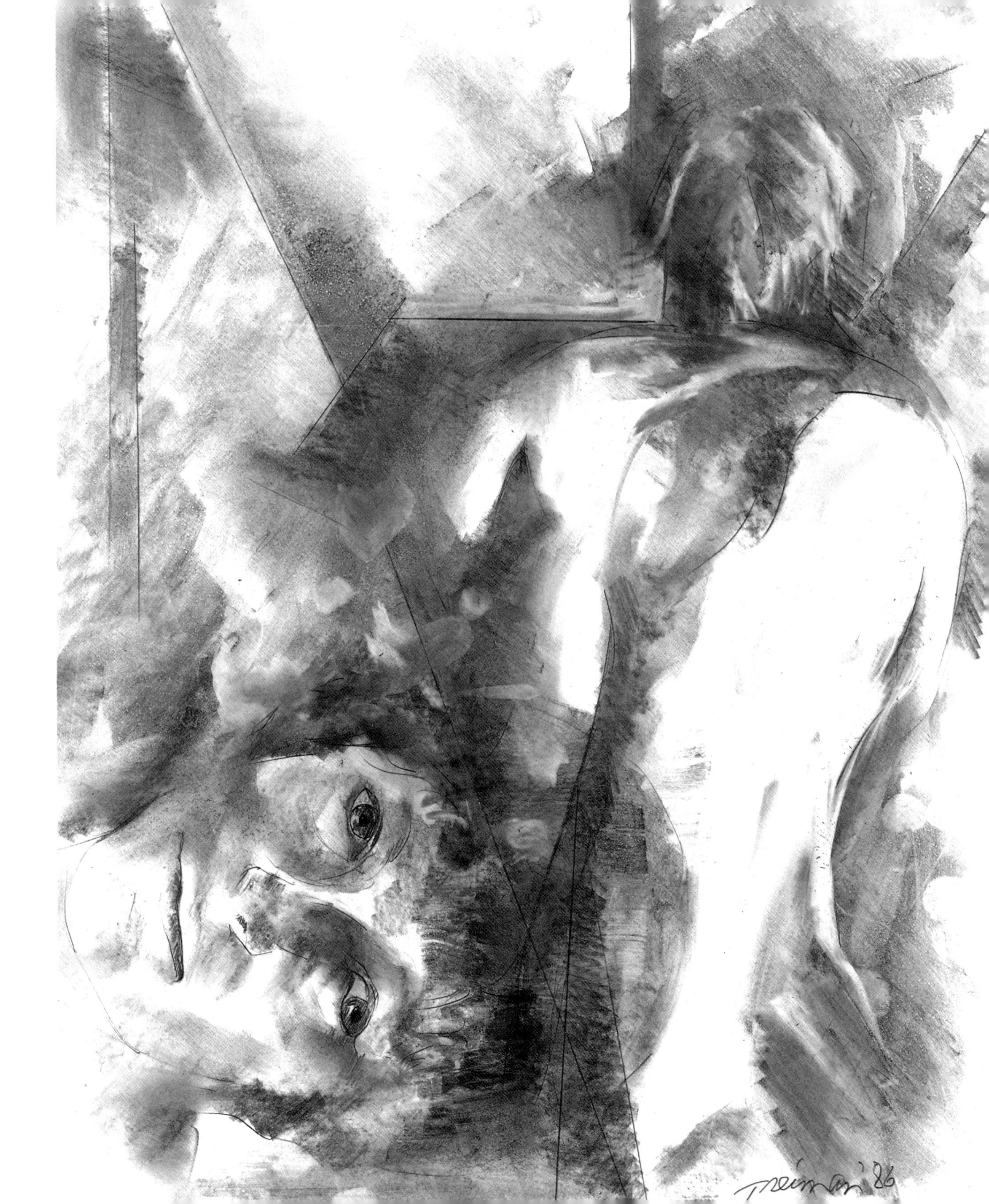

STUDY FOR THE PAINTING
"THE NUDE OUT WEST"
Pastel
1987
Collection of Robert Henning, Jr.
and Brian E. Stenfors, Santa Barbara, California

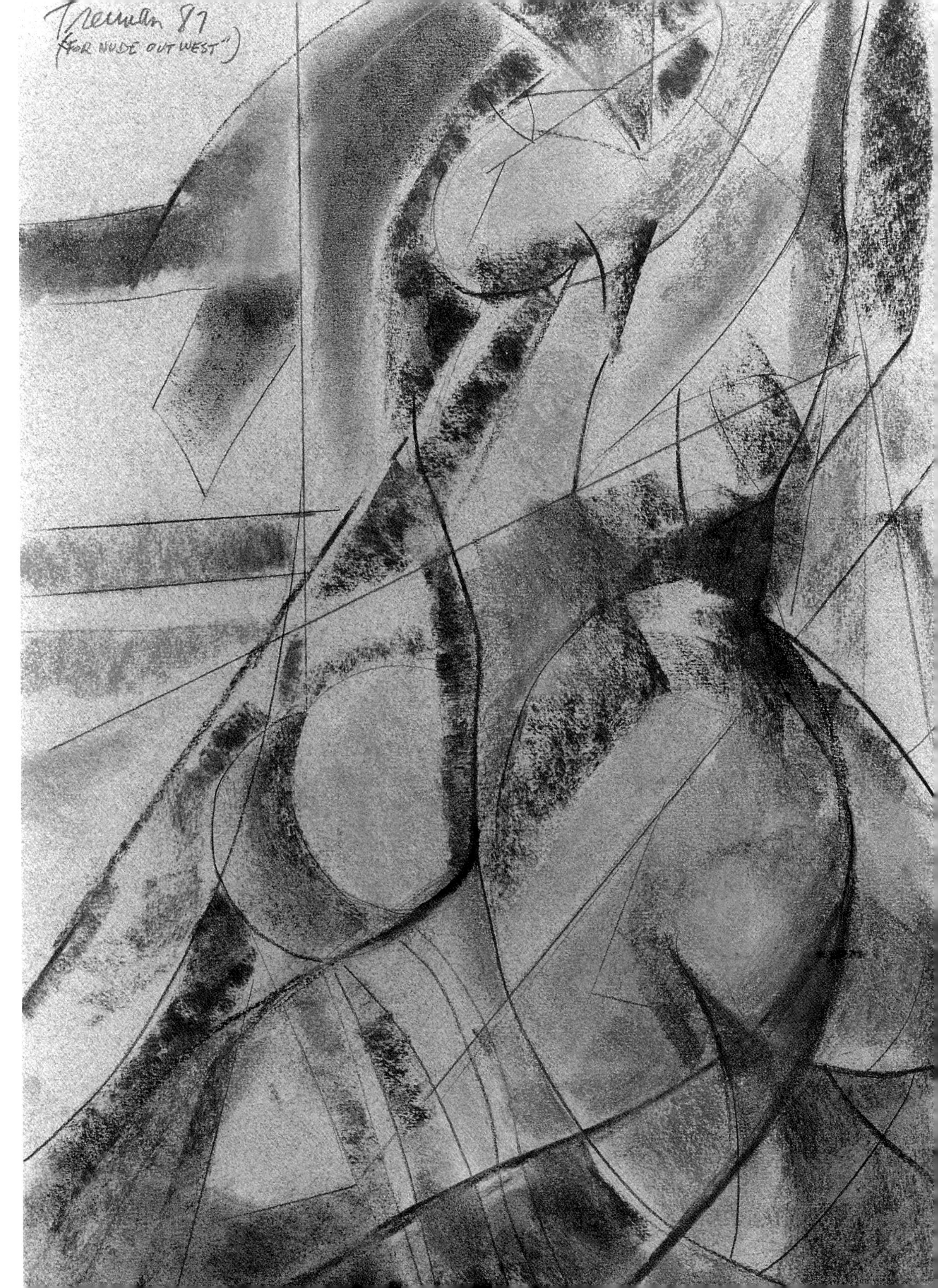
87
("FOR NUDE OUT WEST")

CATALOGUE OF THE EXHIBITION

DRAWINGS

1. *RECLINING MALE FIGURE IN STUDIO*
Pencil
1969, 13¾ × 9½
Courtesy of the Artist

2. *SHEET OF STUDIES*
Pencil and red ink
1969, 10 × 7½
Courtesy of the Artist

3. *TWO STUDIES OF A MODEL*
Red ink
1969, 10 × 7½
Courtesy of the Artist

4. *STUDY FOR PIER PEOPLE II*
Pencil
1975, 18½ × 29½
Collection of Mrs. Owen Fairweather
Barrington, Illinois

5. *STUDY FOR "BIG BONNARD AND ME TWICE"*
Pastel and pencil
1977, 30 × 22
Collection of Mr. and Mrs. Alan D. Levy
Los Angeles, California

6. *STUDY OF A MAN*
Charcoal
1977, 30 × 22
Courtesy of Fairweather Hardin Gallery
Chicago, Illinois

7. *PORTRAIT OF B.D.*
Charcoal and chalk
1977, 30 × 22
Courtesy of the Artist

8. *STUDIES OF DIANA*
Pencil
1977, 29½ × 22¼
Courtesy of the Artist

9. *STUDY FOR TURNER AND ME*
Pencil and ink
1978, 30½ × 22¼
Courtesy of Fairweather Hardin Gallery
Chicago, Illinois

10. *STUDY FOR DEGAS, CASSATT AND ME*
Pastel and pencil
1979, 22¼ × 29
Collection of Mr. and Mrs. Alan D. Levy
Los Angeles, California

11. *SHOWGIRL WITH RED HEADDRESS*
Pastel on black paper
1980, 39 × 28¾
Courtesy of Tortue Gallery
Santa Monica, California

12. *MAN IN BLUE DERBY*
Pastel on black paper
1980, 23½ × 17½
Courtesy of Tortue Gallery
Santa Monica, California

13. *TYCOON*
Pastel on black paper
1980, 24 × 33
Courtesy of Tortue Gallery
Santa Monica, California

14. *WHITE HEADDRESS*
Pastel on green paper
1980, 24 × 19
Courtesy of Tortue Gallery
Santa Monica, California

15. *STUDY FOR TIEPOLO AND ME*
Pencil, watercolor, and colored pencils
1981, 28 × 24
Courtesy of the Artist

16. *THE MEASURE OF ALL THINGS IS MAN*
Pastel and pencil
1982, 33 × 25
Collection of Esther Sparks, Chicago, Illinois

17. *PLUMED HELMET (STUDY FOR THE PARTING)*
Pencil and pastel
1982, 30¼ × 21¾
Collection of Memorial Art Gallery of the
University of Rochester, New York;
Anonymous Gift

18. *THE GREY HAND*
Pastel and pencil
1983, 28 × 20½
Collection of Mr. and Mrs. Alan D. Levy
Los Angeles, California

19. *SELF-PORTRAIT WITH WHITE HAT*
Pastel and pencil
1983, 33⅛ × 25⅛
Courtesy of Fairweather Hardin Gallery
Chicago, Illinois

20. *JOKER WITH MASK (MASKED JOKERS)*
Colored pencils
1984, 18 × 15
Collection of Judith Taylor
Los Angeles, California

21. *SEATED JOKER AND SELF PORTRAIT*
Colored pencils and pencil
1984, 18 × 15
Collection of Richard and Frances Luban
Los Angeles, California

22. *WRESTLING JOKERS*
Colored pencils
1984, 18 × 15
Courtesy of Tortue Gallery
Santa Monica, California

23. *THE ROCK AND THE RAM*
Charcoal, pastel, pencil and colored pencils
1984, 18 × 15
Courtesy of Schmidt-Bingham Gallery
New York, New York

24. *THE RIDER*
Pastel and pencil
1984, 33⅛ × 25⅛
Collection of Judd Hammack
Santa Monica, California

25. *INCIDENT I*
Pastel and pencil
1984, 33 × 25
Collection of Darryl and Doris Curran
Los Angeles, California

26. *JOKER WITH BLUE STRIPED JACKET*
Pastel and colored pencils
1984, 24 × 21
Courtesy of Tortue Gallery
Santa Monica, California

27. *ROSE VI*
Pastel and charcoal
1985, 30 × 25
Collection of Dr. and Mrs. Aaron Nisenson
Santa Barbara, California

28. *ROSE VII*
Pastel and charcoal
1985, 30 × 22
Courtesy of Tortue Gallery
Santa Monica, California

29. *ROSE VIII*
Pastel and charcoal
1985, 30 × 22
Courtesy of Tortue Gallery
Santa Monica, California

30. *ROSE IX*
Pastel and charcoal
1985, 30 × 22
Collection of Judith Taylor
Los Angeles, California

31. *ROSE X*
Pastel and charcoal
1986, 30 × 22
Collection of Donald M. Treiman
Los Angeles, California

32. *NINE STUDIES FOR THE PAINTING "THE NUDE OUT WEST"*
Charcoal, pastel, pencil and ink
1986–87
Courtesy of the Artist

33. *STUDY FOR THE PAINTING "THE NUDE OUT WEST"*
Pastel
1987
Collection of Robert Henning, Jr. and Brian E. Stenfors
Santa Barbara, California

PAINTINGS

1. *VIEW OF ANY ARRIVAL*
   Oil on canvas
   1964, 40 × 40
   Collection of Joseph Cecil
   Chicago, Illinois

2. *THE SECRET*
   Oil on canvas
   1965–66, 40 × 40
   Collection of California State University
   Foundation, Northridge, California;
   Art Collection Commission

3. *THE BIRTHDAY PARTY*
   Oil on canvas
   1966–67, 70 × 70
   Collection of Dr. and Mrs. Aaron Nisenson
   Santa Barbara, California

4. *STANDING MAN*
   Oil on canvas
   1968–69, 40 × 30
   Collection of David Huntington Cherish
   Los Angeles, California

5. *YELLOW LAMPSHADE*
   Oil on canvas
   1968–69, 40 × 40
   Collection of Carol and Charles Greenberg
   Long Beach, California

6. *THE BOUQUET*
   Oil on canvas
   1969, 36 × 24
   Collection of Harry W. Saunders
   Los Angeles, California

7. *ANOMIE*
   Oil on canvas
   1969–70, 70 × 70
   Collection of Whitney Museum of Art, New York;
   Gift of an anonymous donor (71.227)

8. *THE ADVENTURE*
   Oil on canvas
   1970, 48 × 60
   Collection of Ronald Harrison Cooper
   and Nancy E. Cooper
   Los Angeles, California

9. *SELF-PORTRAIT/COWBOY KEN*
   Oil on canvas
   1970–71, 24 × 36
   Collection of the City of Los Angeles, California;
   Permanent Art Collection

10. *SWIMMERS ANTIBES, TOPANGA*
    Oil on canvas
    1971, 24 × 48
    Collection of Long Beach Museum of Art
    Long Beach, California

11. *DEAR FRIENDS*
    Oil on canvas
    1972, 70 × 70
    Collection of Mr. and Mrs. Maurice B. Wilson
    Carlsbad, California

12. *THOMAS EAKINS MODELING IN CALIFORNIA*
    Oil on canvas
    1974, 70 × 70
    Collection of Mark E.B. Pinney
    Garrison, New York

13. *THE BIG SARGENT*
    Oil on canvas
    1975, 70 × 70
    Collection of Dr. S. Sanford and Charlene
    Kornblum, Beverly Hills, California

14. *BIG LAUTREC AND DOUBLE SELF-PORTRAIT*
    Oil on canvas
    1975–76, 70 × 70
    Collection of Kemper Group Art
    Long Grove, Illinois

15. *ROSE, BONNARD AND ARTIST TWICE*
    Oil on canvas
    1977, 70 × 70
    Pritzker Family Collection
    Chicago, Illinois

16. *DEGAS, CASSATT AND ME*
    Oil on canvas
    1979, 70 × 70
    Collection of Harry W. Saunders
    Los Angeles, California

17. *PAGE TWO*
Oil on canvas
1979, 70 × 50
Collection of Mr. and Mrs. John A. Pritzker
San Francisco, California

18. *MONET AND ME*
Oil on canvas
1980, 80 × 60
Collection of Security Pacific Corporation
Los Angeles, California

19. *DEJEUNER*
Oil on canvas
1981, 80 × 60
Collection of Harry W. Saunders
Los Angeles, California

20. *TIEPOLO AND ME*
Oil on canvas
1981, 70 × 70
Collection of Richard and Frances Luban
Los Angeles, California

21. *GIVERNY REVISITED*
Oil on canvas
1982, 80 × 34
Courtesy of the Artist

22. *SELF-PORTRAIT IN TITUS' HAT*
Oil on canvas
1983, 78 × 40
Collection of Mrs. Owen Fairweather
Barrington, Illinois

23. *THANATOPSIS*
Oil on canvas
1983, 70 × 70
Collection of Harry W. Saunders
Los Angeles, California

24. *HERCULES ARCADIAN STAG*
Oil on canvas
1983, 70 × 70
Collection of Peter and Sharon Elkington
Pacific Palisades, California

25. *HERCULES AND CERBERUS*
Oil on canvas
1983, 40 × 30
Courtesy of Tortue Gallery
Santa Monica, California

26. *THE PARTING*
Oil on canvas
1983, 80 × 60
Collection of Memorial Art Gallery of the University of Rochester, New York;
Marion Stratton Gould Fund

27. *SAILING AWAY (TILTED ME)*
Oil on canvas
1985–86, 48 × 30
Collection of Dr. S. Sanford and Charlene Kornblum, Beverly Hills, California

28. *WIT'S END*
Oil on canvas
1986, 70 × 70
Collection of Ronald Harrison Cooper and Nancy E. Cooper, Los Angeles, California

29. *FRIENDS AND STRANGERS*
Oil on canvas
1986, 70 × 70
Collection of Mr. and Mrs. Tom Pritzker
Chicago, Illinois

30. *THE NUDE OUT WEST*
Oil on canvas
1987, 70 × 70
Collection of Mr. and Mrs. John A. Pritzker
San Francisco, California

Joyce Treiman has often been described as one of the premier painters in the United States. "No contemporary American artist", writes art critic Theodore Wolff, "can paint better or more exultantly than she . . ." Indeed, Wolff claims that Treiman has "produced some of the most provocative and beautiful paintings and drawings of the past two or three decades".

Such critical acclaim, however, does not refute the fact that Treiman's work is relatively unknown to curators, art historians and the museum-going public in general. A complete individualist, Treiman has steadfastly created a highly personal art independent of the trends of the moment. Her career, in many ways, is reminiscent of those of Edwin Dickinson and Fairfield Porter, two major American artists who belatedly received critical recognition and acceptance. Like Dickinson, Treiman is a representational painter who freely manipulates and transforms reality; and, like Porter, she fully understands the underpinnings of modernism while adhering to an independent artistic vision.

When Minimalism, Hard Edge, and other forms of abstract painting were in vogue, Treiman reveled in her mastery of the human form and painted monumental canvases that reflected her belief that art must refer to human aspirations, needs, and ideals. "I'm a humanist" she declared, "I care about the human spirit and about great art". Her deep and abiding interest in the art of the past (she once stated, "I have always carried great paintings around in my head") enables her also to dismiss the current trend of "appropriation". Treiman's cultural memory runs deep and goes well beyond mere quotation. Nourished by what Yeats calls the "monuments of unageing intellect", she absorbs the technical brilliance and broad humanistic concerns of such masters as Rembrandt, Goya, Monet, Bonnard and Eakins. "The only road to authenticity", notes critic Robert Hughes, "lies through a deep and continuous experience of what has already been done. There is no deep art without profound historical awareness". In her best work, Treiman fully expresses her own epoch while maintaining an instinctive and true feeling for the highest standards of the past. Her work is always authentic and often profound.

The exhibition *Joyce Treiman: Friends and Strangers* celebrates an art of human situations. From Venice, California to Giverny, France; from bourgeois parlors to ringside at Las Vegas; and from the "anomie" of empty lives to the joys of the creative life, we witness an artist who delights in the diversity of "la comedie humaine". Even *Thomas Eakins Modeling in California* and *Hercules and the Arcadian Stag*, purely imaginative compositions, seem real incidents observed by the artist because they intimately involve her basic feelings and ideas about art and life. Whether critical observer or active participant, Treiman is the chief protagonist throughout *Friends and Strangers.* She labors with Hercules *(Hercules and the Nemean Lion)*, cavorts with Monet and John Singer Sargent *(Monet and*

Me; The Big Sargent), rides horses "out west" *(Self-Portrait with Cowboy)* and confronts her mortality bravely *(Thanatopsis)* if somewhat skeptically *(The Parting)*. As Wolff has correctly surmised, very little happens in the artist's emotional and intellectual life that does not find itself "transformed into line, paint and color, and projected onto canvas and paper".

Perhaps *The Nude Out West*, painted in 1987, can be viewed as a recapitulation, a summary, of Treiman's work over the past two decades. It is a painting, for example, that combines the artist's interest in portraiture, landscape and monumental narrative allegory. In addition, many of the characters in the painting are old and "Dear Friends". Cowboys and other images of the west, including the artist in western and Indian attire, recall her equestrian portraits of the 1960s and the Americana series of the early 70s. Even the cross-eyed buffalo brings to mind the endearing images of animals that have appeared in her work from the beginning. The "beautiful people" embarking on transatlantic voyages and the mischievous Joker have been the primary subjects in recent years. Finally, Treiman's poignant tribute to her beloved mother, Rose, is continued, both literally and symbolically, in this painterly reprise.

The Nude Out West, a composition of dramatic contrasts, is equally complex in form and structure. Space is at once illusionistic and flat; paint refined and "brut"; surfaces transparent and opaque. Multiple perspectives and light sources, in addition to blurred, overlapping and intersecting images, further enhance Treiman's unusual approach to visual reality. Her figurative premise is both challenged and enlivened by the abstract stylistic references to Kandinsky, Delauney and Archipenko that swirl through the composition.

The Nude Out West, like much of Treiman's oeuvre, is daring and imaginative in form and often elusive and enigmatic in content. She shares with Walter Murch, an artist she greatly admires, the belief that art must achieve a "peculiar beauty" that strikes "a chord inside, deep inside one, a chord that is inexplainable . . .". Treiman admirably fulfills Wordsworth's definition of the true artist. She possesses a lively sensibility, enthusiasm and tenderness. She is pleased with her own passions and volitions and rejoices more than others in the spirit of life that is in her. She contemplates similar passions manifested in the world around her and is habitually compelled to create them when she does not find them. Like Lear and Cordelia, Joyce Treiman has taken upon herself the mystery of things and, in the process, has become one of God's spies.

Grant Holcomb
Director, Memorial Art Gallery
Rochester, New York

THE ADVENTURE
Oil on canvas
1970, 48 × 60
Collection of Ronald Harrison Cooper
and Nancy E. Cooper
Los Angeles, California

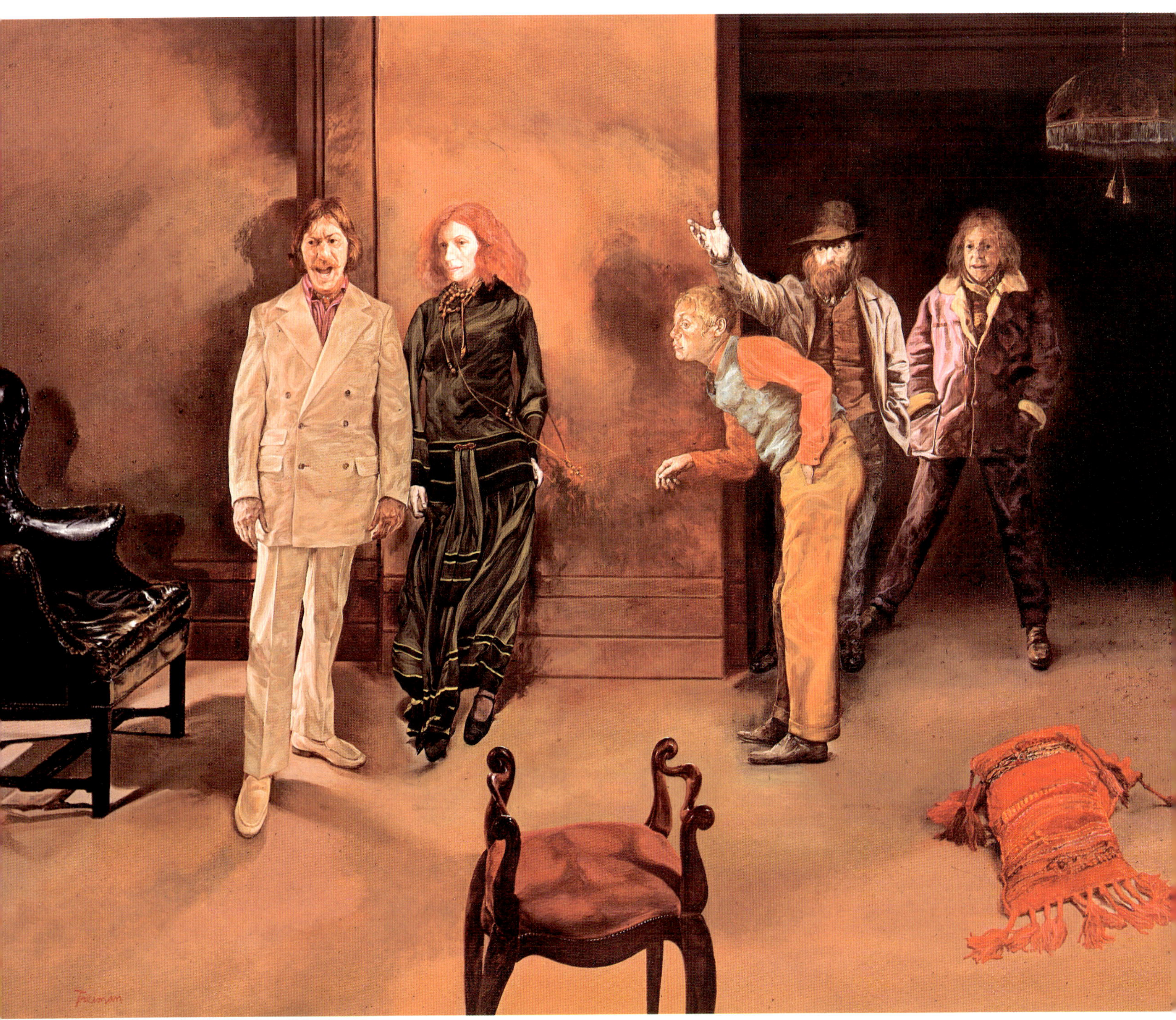

DEAR FRIENDS
Oil on canvas
1972, 70 × 70
Collection of Mr. and Mrs. Maurice B. Wilson
Carlsbad, California

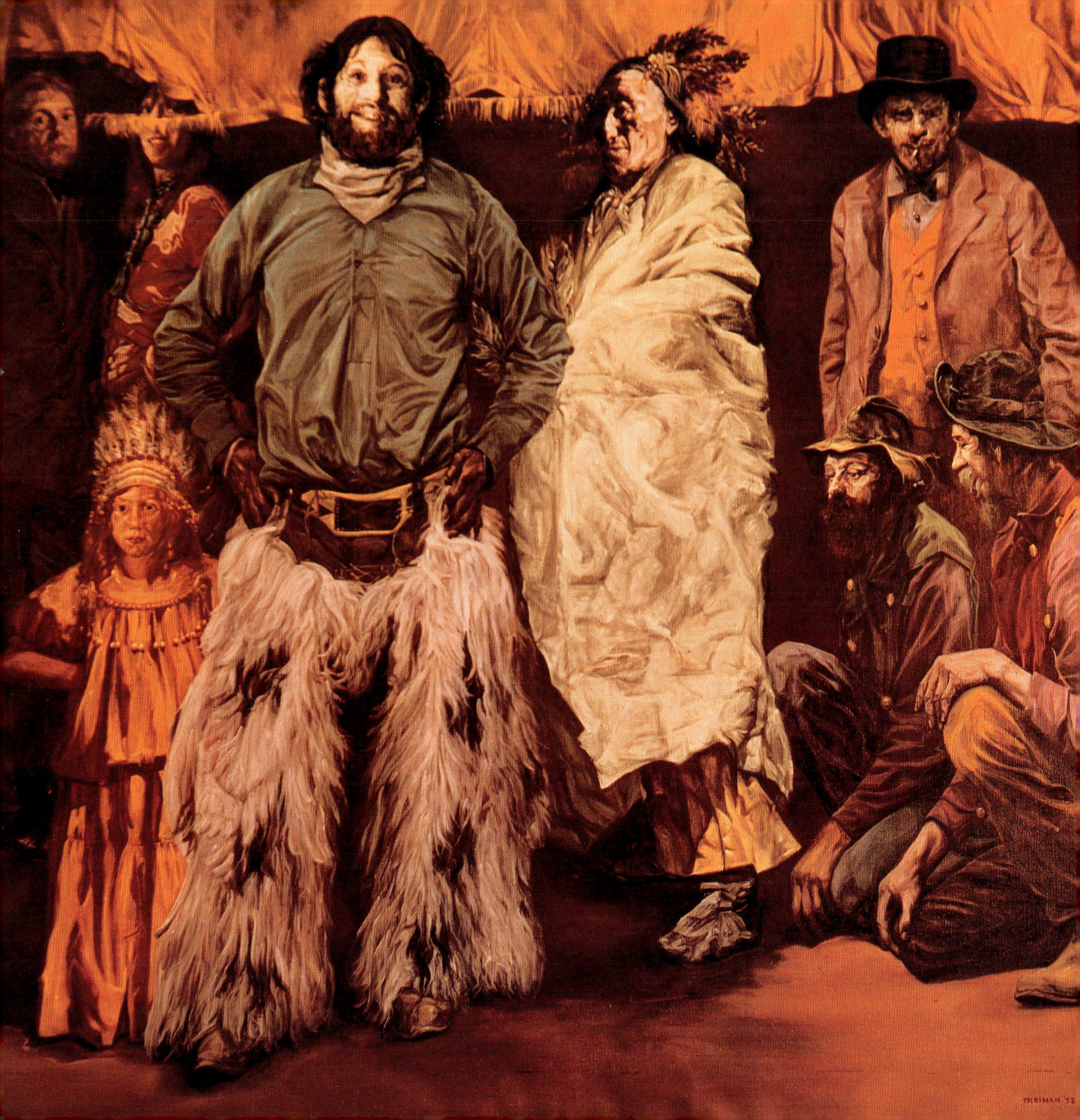
TREIMAN '72

THE PARTING
Oil on canvas
1983, 80 × 60
Collection of Memorial Art Gallery of the
University of Rochester, New York;
Marion Stratton Gould Fund

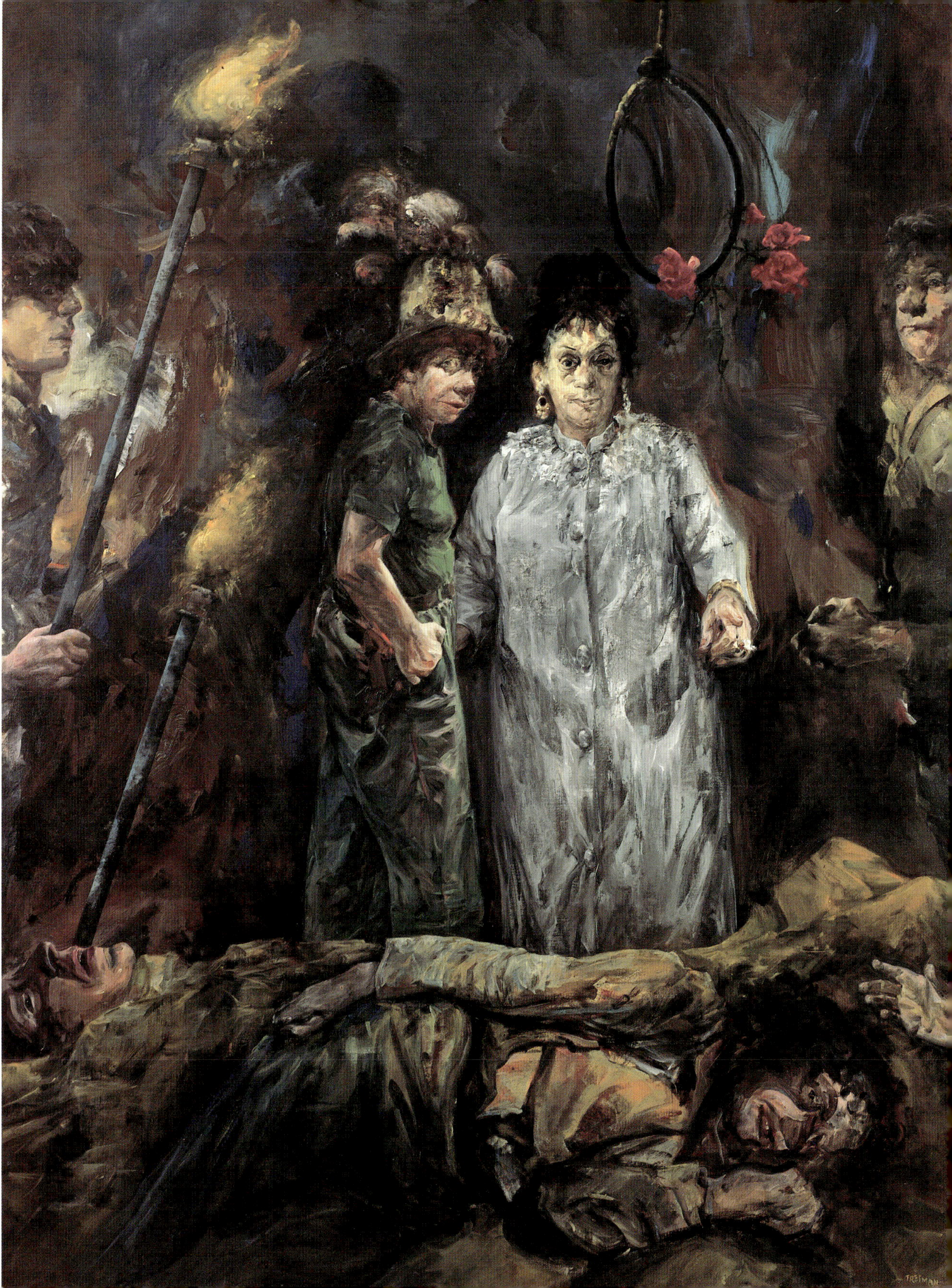

THANATOPSIS
Oil on canvas
1983, 70 × 70
Collection of Harry W. Saunders
Los Angeles, California

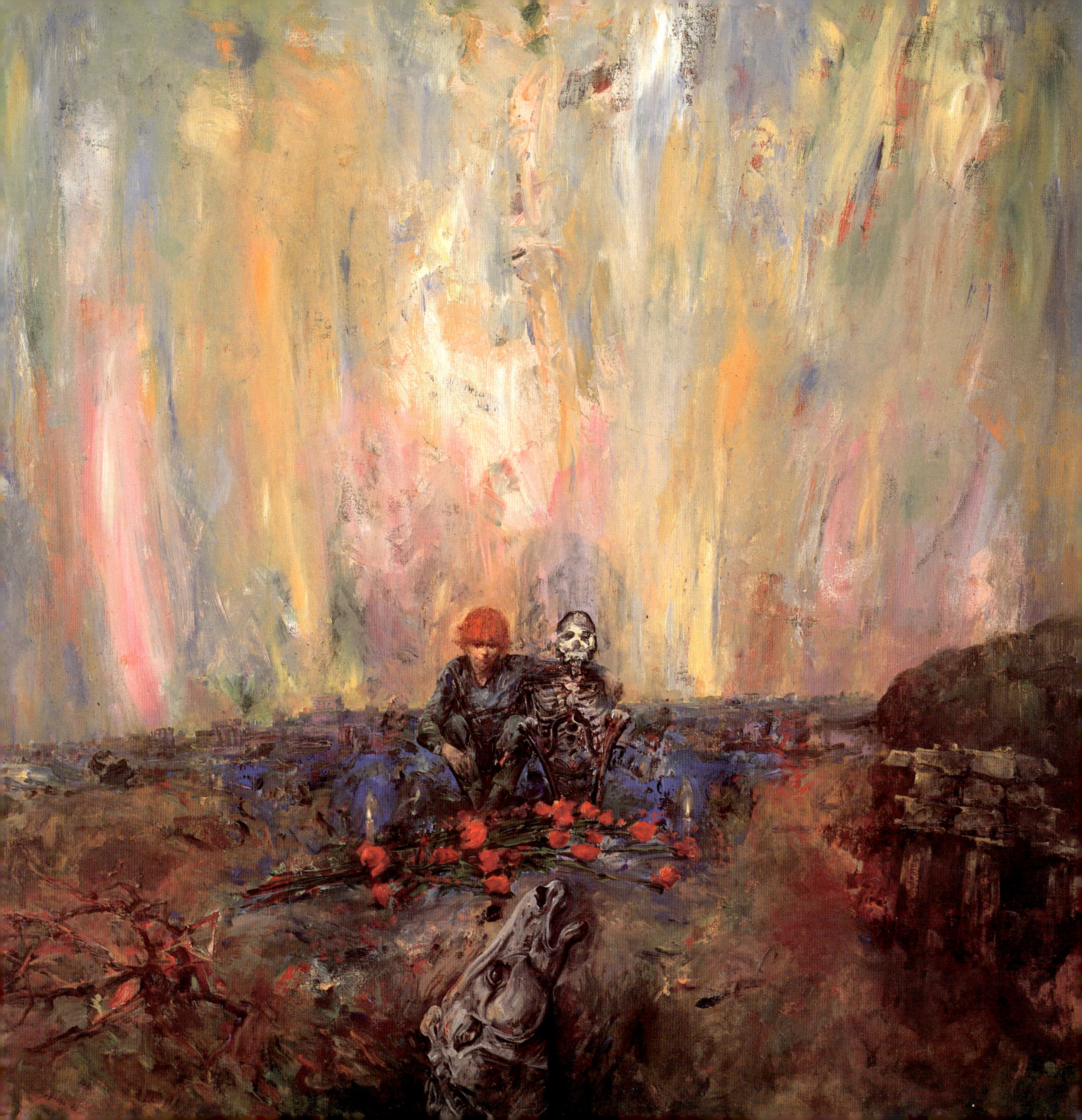

SAILING AWAY (TILTED ME)
Oil on canvas
1985–86, 48 × 30
Collection of Dr. S. Sanford and Charlene Kornblum
Beverly Hills, California

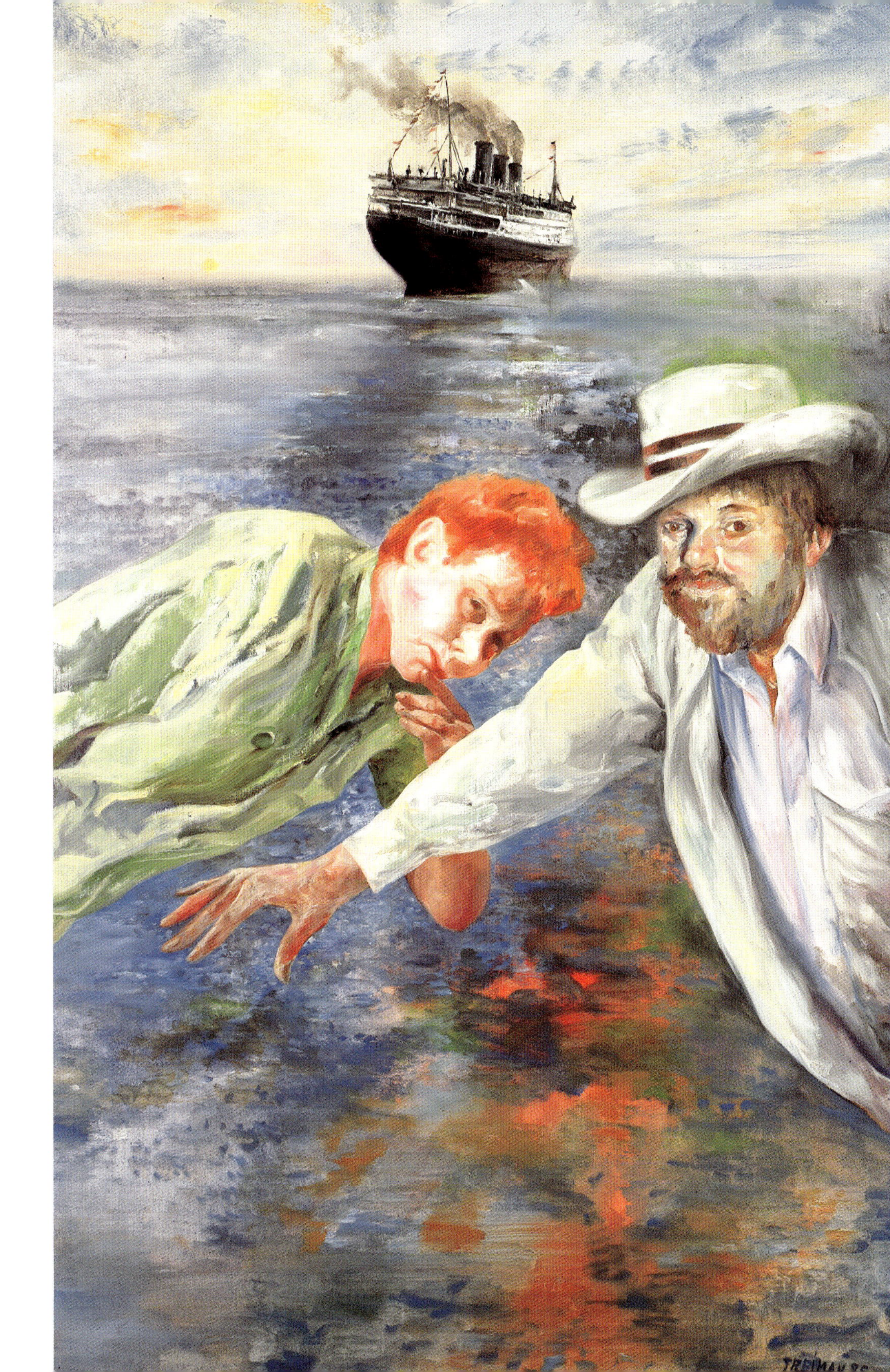

WIT'S END
Oil on canvas
1986, 70 × 70
Collection of Ronald Harrison Cooper and
Nancy E. Cooper, Los Angeles, California

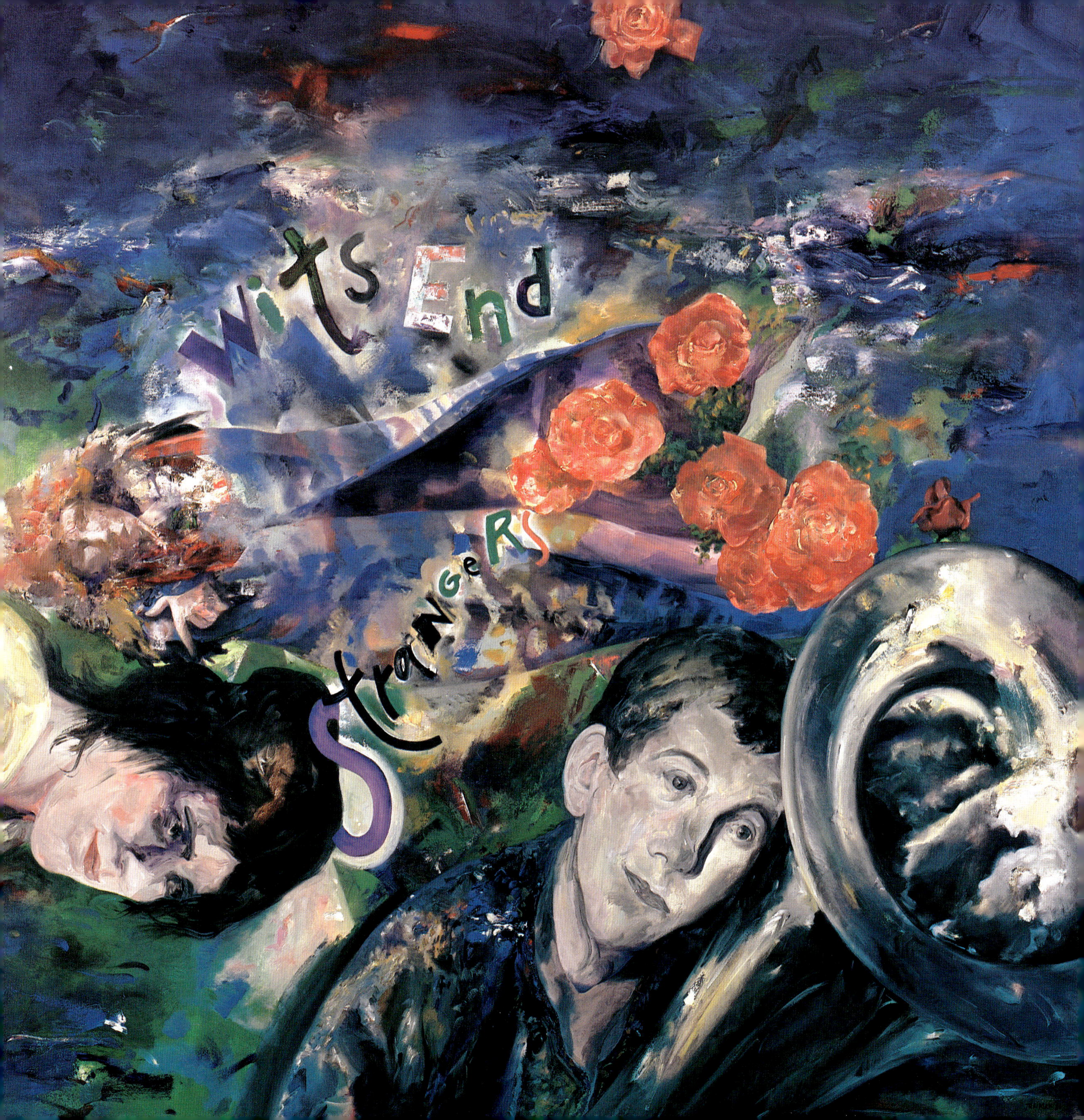
Wits End
Strangers

THE NUDE OUT WEST
Oil on canvas
1987, 70 × 70
Collection of Mr. and Mrs. John A. Pritzker
San Francisco, California

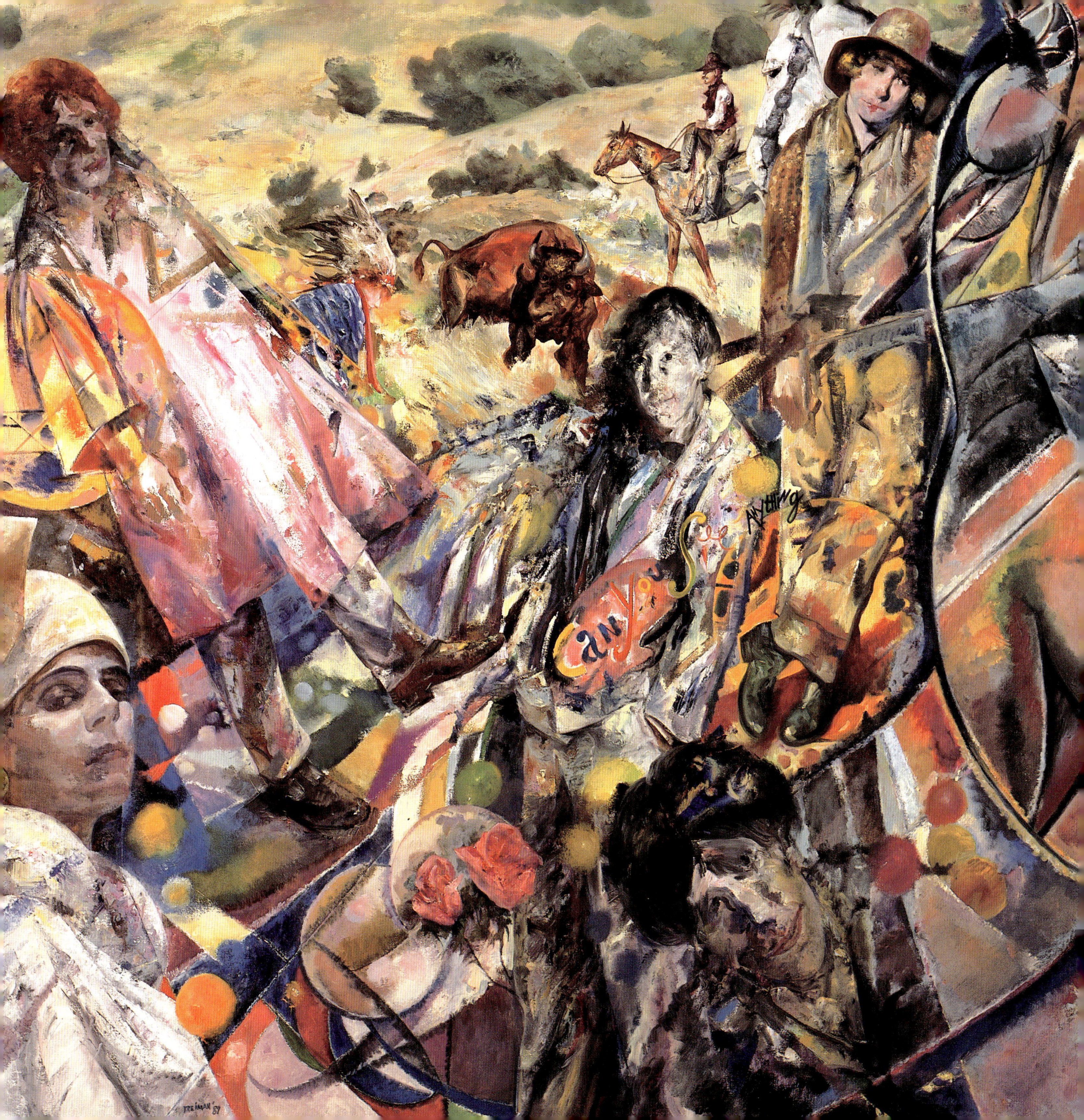
Can You See Anything
FREIMAN '87

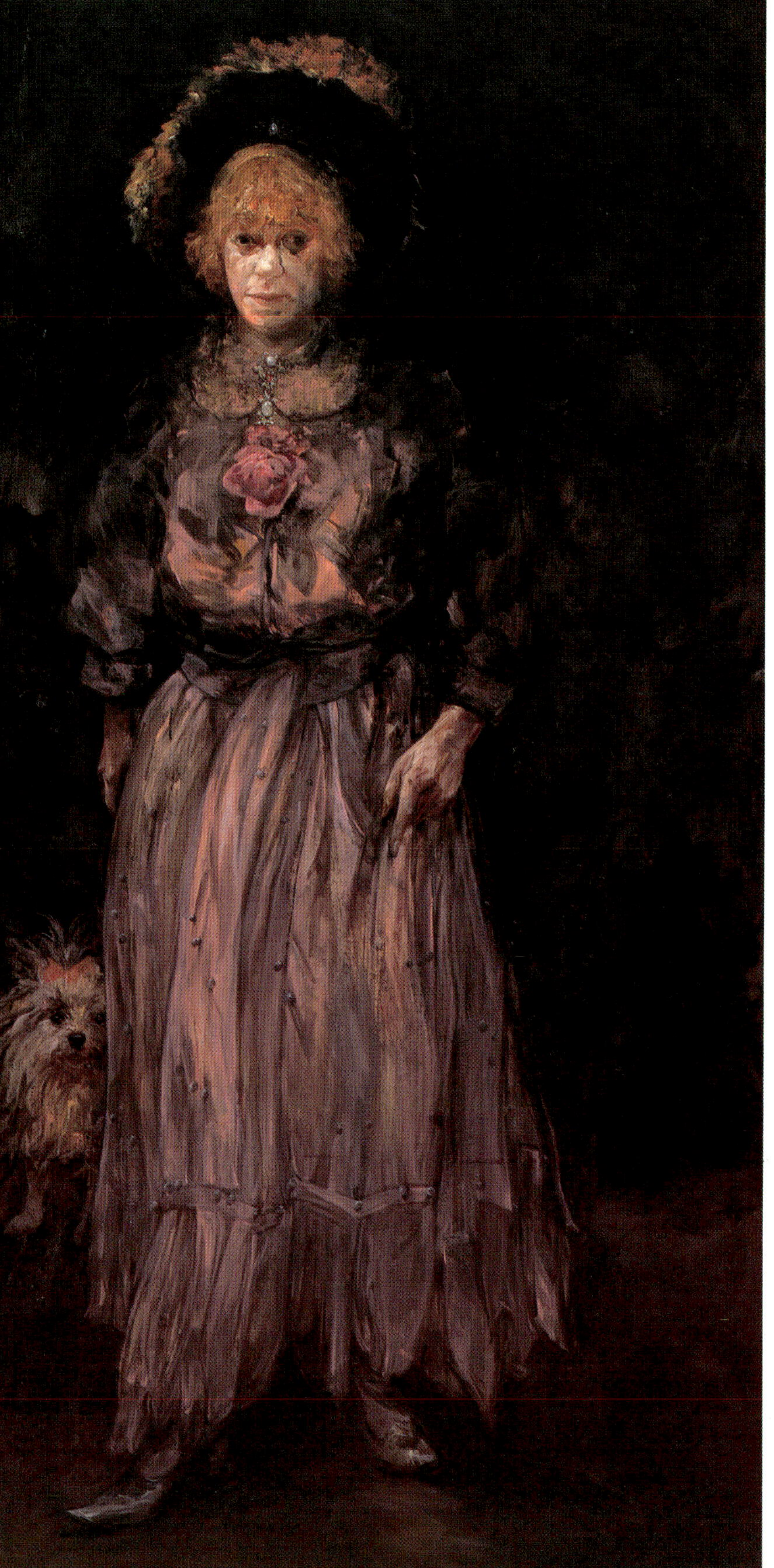

SELF-PORTRAIT IN TITUS' HAT
Oil on canvas
1983, 78 × 40
Collection of Mrs. Owen Fairweather
Barrington, Illinois